FAITH AS A LIFELINE

Faith, Survival, and the Light
Beyond Suicide

HALIMAH JORDAN

Al Yusra
9582 Tara Boulevard
Jonesboro GA 30236
United States of America

Library of Congress Control Number: 2025910320
ISBN: 979-8-9989764-0—7 (Paperback)

Email: halimah@alyusra.com
www.alyusra.com

AL YUSRA
www.alyusra.com

TABLE OF CONTENTS

Introduction 1

Chapter 1: The Quiet Weight: What Suicide Really
Looks Like 4

Chapter 2: Faith as a Lifeline 16

Chapter 3: When You're the One Hurting 22

Chapter 4: Building Your Hope Plan 31

Chapter 5: The Many Faces of Despair 44

Chapter 6: What the Mind Believes, the Body Feels 68

Chapter 7: Creating a Life Worth Staying For 74

Chapter 8: You Were Never Alone...............................80

Farewell Message to the Reader 87

Appendix..89

References 103

Acknowledgments 105

Faith as a Lifeline

Faith, Survival, and the Light Beyond Suicide

INTRODUCTION

"You're Here, and That's Enough"

Dear Reader,

Before you turn another page, take a deep breath, you made it here and that means a lot to me. That means something. Maybe everything.

Maybe you're holding this book with trembling hands. Maybe you're here because somebody you loved ended their life. Maybe you're here because you are the one who is barely hanging on. Or maybe you're standing in the sacred space between heartbreak and healing, trying to make sense of what cannot be undone.

Whatever brought you here, I want you to know that you are not alone.

I wrote this book as I have seen the long shadows that grief can cast. As a mother, teacher, and woman of faith, I have sat with people in their pain. I've witnessed the silence that surrounds suicide. I've felt the weight of questions without answers. This book was born out of compassion for those who have felt that their sorrow had no home and no words.

If you're looking for perfect answers, I won't pretend to have them. This book is not here to fix you; it's meant to sit with you on your journey to a peaceful life. It will walk with you through your grief, your confusion, and your moments of anger and quiet disbelief. It will offer stories, reflections, gentle guidance, and a reminder that your pain matters. You're here and that's enough.

With love and peace,

Halimah Jordan

Your pain is not
the end of your story.

It's a doorway — and
mercy is already waiting
on the other side.

CHAPTER 1

The Quiet Weight: What Suicide Really Looks Like

---∞---

Introduction

Suicide rarely looks like what most people imagine.

It's not always someone crying for help or openly showing despair.

Often, it's hidden beneath smiles, polite conversations, and busy schedules.

It's a silent, quiet weight carried in hearts we never thought to check.

In the book *Life Inside My Mind* by Jessica Burkhart, the author reflects on how often people wear a fake happy face — not for themselves, but to make others more comfortable. She urges us to do the opposite: **to be honest about our pain.** When someone asks how you are, she says, tell them the truth. If you're not okay, say so. People can't support you if they don't know you're struggling.

Don't mask your pain behind a smile. Let others see your real face. And when someone else opens up — when they say, "I'm not okay" — **listen. Don't dismiss them. Believe them.**

You might be handing them the emotional flashlight they need to survive a long, dark night.

Understanding what suicidal ideation really looks like is the first step to breaking stigma, opening conversations, and God willing, saving lives.

Myths and Truths About Suicidal Ideation

Myth:

"If someone were suicidal, they would tell someone."

Truth:

Many people who struggle with suicidal thoughts hide them out of shame, fear of burdening others, or fear of judgment. Silence is not safety. Silence is often pain.

Myth:

"Only people with obvious depression think about suicide."

Truth:

Suicidal ideation can affect people who seem high-functioning — working, studying, parenting — while silently battling hopelessness inside.

Myth:

"Talking about suicide makes it more likely."

Truth:

Talking about suicide with compassion reduces risk.

Silence and denial make people feel even more isolated.

Why People Hide It

For people of faith, the struggle to talk about suicidal thoughts is even heavier.

- Fear of being judged as weak in faith.
- Fear of bringing shame to their family.
- Cultural stigma: "We don't talk about these things."

In many faith communities, mental health is still deeply misunderstood.

Instead of being offered help and mercy, those struggling are often met with suspicion or blame.

But in Islam, Prophet Muhammad (peace be upon him) taught compassion, not cruelty.

He said:

"Make matters easy, and do not make them difficult;
give glad tidings and do not make people run away."
(Sahih al-Bukhari 69)

We must be the voices that say:

"You are not bad. You are not weak. You are hurting — and hurting needs healing, not shame."

Why "But They Looked Fine" Is Misleading

One of the most heartbreaking things people say after a suicide is:

"But they looked fine."

The truth is:

- Some people learn to hide their pain very well.
- Some don't want to burden others.
- Some are waiting for someone to notice without them having to beg.

Pain does not always show on the surface.

It hides behind busy lives, friendly smiles, and "I'm fine" answers.

If someone crosses your mind — reach out.

A simple "How are you really?" could save a life.

Suicide: Truth vs. Stigma

Islam values every single life, no matter how wounded.

- Suicide is forbidden (haram) in Islam.
- But Islam also teaches that despair is a human weakness, not a curse.
- God is the Most Merciful, the Constant Forgiver.

The Prophet Muhammad (peace be upon him) said:

"When God completed the creation, He wrote in His Book which is with Him on His Throne: 'My Mercy overcomes My Anger.'" **(Sahih al-Bukhari 3194)**

This means: even in tragedy, we turn to God's mercy.

Islam encourages us to:

- Stop the act of suicide.
- Heal the pain that leads to it.
- Treat those struggling with mercy, prayer, and practical help — not cruelty or judgment.

Suicide is not a "faith issue." It is a pain issue — one that Islam teaches us to meet with *compassion, counsel,* and *connection.*

A Quiet Crisis, By the Numbers

While suicide is a personal, spiritual struggle, it's also a growing public reality — and certain groups are suffering in silence more than others.

Recent studies show:

- Suicide is now the second leading cause of death for youth ages 10–24.

- Black youth have seen a 36% increase in suicide rates in just a few years.

- **American Indian and Alaska Native populations** have the highest rates of suicide among all racial and ethnic groups.

- Among girls ages 8–12, suicide is rising faster than ever before.

- Nearly 41% of LGBTQ+ youth say they have seriously considered suicide in the past year.

- Men die by suicide nearly four times more often than women, though women attempt it more often.

- Older adults, especially white males over 65, have the highest suicide completion rates of any group.

This is not a small problem. It's a quiet storm affecting our children, our elders, our neighbors, and our communities of faith.

The Role of Faith and Belief

Religious belief — particularly regular spiritual practice and community connection — is consistently shown to protect against suicide.

- Muslims, on average, have lower reported suicide rates compared to other groups, though cultural stigma and underreporting remain issues.

- A 2020 Harvard study found that people who attend religious services weekly have up to 5 times lower risk of dying by suicide.

- People without any faith or spiritual anchor often report higher levels of hopelessness, isolation, and despair.

But let this be clear:

Suicide is not just about faith.

It is also about trauma, biology, loneliness, and the need to be seen and supported.

Still — **faith offers a lifeline** that many don't realize is within reach.

What This Means for Us

If we want to save lives, we have to speak the truth:

- Faith helps.
- Community matters.

- Silence kills.

- And stigma has no place in spaces meant to heal.

Suicide isn't just a crisis of the mind — it's also a spiritual wound.

And wounds don't heal when they're hidden.

The Test Beyond This Life

Many people who consider suicide are searching for a way out of pain.

They believe that if they end their life, the suffering will end and their problems will disappear.

But will they really?

What many forget is that this life is not the end — it's only the beginning.

Every major revelation — the Bible, the Torah, and the final revelation, the Qur'an — teaches that there will be a Day of Judgment.

A day when every action, every intention, every moment of patience or despair will be accounted for.

There is life after death.

There is accountability after this test.

If we truly understood — with absolute certainty — that suicide is not an escape but a transition into another, eternal life, would we still choose to end this one so soon?

Death ends the test of this life, yes.

But it does not end existence.

It simply moves us forward into the next chapter — a chapter that has no ending, no dying, no second chances.

This life is short — 70 or 80 years on average.

But the next life is forever.

We don't want to meet our Lord having surrendered in despair,forgetting that He promised:

"God does not burden a soul beyond what it can bear."
(Qur'an 2:286)

If He brought you to this moment, He can bring you through it.

Hold on.

Hope is near.

And the eternal story of your soul is still being written.

Pause and Reflect

If I knew that my soul would live forever, how would I choose to end this test?

Faith, Belonging, and the Will to Stay

In every soul lies a search for meaning. For some, faith is that compass — a lifeline in the darkest hour. For others, that compass may feel broken, distant, or never fully held.

Research shows something many of us already feel: those with strong spiritual or religious identities are less likely to die by suicide. In fact, among those who attend religious services regularly, the risk drops even further. The protective nature of faith comes not only from beliefs, but from belonging — to a community, a Creator, and a sense of purpose.

Those who identify as atheist or unaffiliated face significantly higher risks of suicide. This is not a judgment. It's an invitation to reflect on the role that connection — to people, purpose, and possibly to the Divine — can play in healing a fractured heart.

But statistics don't tell the whole story.

They can't explain the tears behind a closed door.

They can't see the man who once believed but now feels nothing.

They can't hear the woman whisper, "I just want the pain to stop."

So this message is not only for believers — it's for the *weary*.

For the *questioning*.

For the ones who lost their faith, or never found it.

There is still hope.

There is still mercy.

There is still a way back — not just to God, but to *yourself*.

Whether you are Muslim, Christian, spiritual-but-not-religious, or searching for something beyond words, know this: **your life matters**. And though the statistics may show who is most at risk, *none of us are immune to despair*.

But none of us are beyond healing, either.

Closing Reflection:

"There is always more to the story than we can see.
Be the one who notices.
Be the one who shows mercy.
Be the one who says, 'You are not alone.'
Because in the quiet weight someone carries — there could be a life waiting to be saved."

Even when your hands
are too tired to pray,
your heart still whispers
hope—and Allah still
hears it.

CHAPTER 2

Faith as a Lifeline

What Keeps Us Here When We Want to Go

When the heart feels crushed, when the pain feels endless, when the world feels too heavy — what keeps us alive?

It is faith.

Sometimes a small, trembling faith. Sometimes a loud, desperate one.

But always, deep inside, a whisper:

"Maybe God still has something for me."

Faith does not erase pain instantly.

But faith gives pain meaning — and meaning gives hope.

Believing that God sees, hears, and loves you — even in the darkest moments — is a lifeline stronger than any chain pulling you downward.

Even when you feel you are hanging by a thread, know this:

The thread is held by God.

Stories of the Prophets: Hardship, Despair, But Never Hopelessness

The Qur'an is not a book of perfect people with perfect lives.

It is a book of struggling souls — just like us — who never gave up hope in God.

Prophet Ayyub (Job) (peace be upon him)

- Lost his health, wealth, family.

- Suffered years of disease and isolation.

- Yet he prayed:

"Indeed, adversity has touched me, and You are the Most Merciful of the merciful."
(Qur'an 21:83)

Prophet Yunus (Jonah), peace be upon him, found himself engulfed in layers of darkness — the night, the ocean, and the belly of a great whale.

In what seemed like complete despair and isolation, he turned to Allah with a heartfelt plea:

"There is no deity except You; exalted are You. Indeed, I have been of the wrongdoers."
(Qur'an 21:87)

Even in the depths, he was not lost — because he remembered his Lord.

Maryam (Mary) (Mother of Jesus – Isa)

- Alone, misunderstood, giving birth under a tree, crying:

"I wish I had died before this and was in oblivion, forgotten."

(Qur'an 19:23)

- But God provided water, shade, and dignity for her.

None of them gave up hope.

Even in crushing loneliness, even in human despair, they turned back to God — and God lifted them.

When Faith Feels Far — and How to Reach Back

There will be days when:

- Prayer feels empty.
- Prayer feels like silence.
- Qur'an feels like distant echoes.

This is normal.

Even strong believers go through droughts of the heart.

When faith feels far:

- **Start small.** Whisper "Astaghfirullah" (May God forgive me) even if you feel numb.

- **Return to the basics.** Pray even if you have to cry through it.

- **Name your pain to God.** Talk to Him like you would a friend.

The Prophet Mohammad (peace be upon him) taught:

*"The most beloved deeds to God are those that are consistent, even if small."***(Sahih al-Bukhari 6464)**

You don't have to climb a mountain of faith today.

You just have to take one small step toward Him — and He promises to come running toward you.

*"If he comes to Me walking, I come to him running."***(Hadith Qudsi, Sahih al-Bukhari 7405)**

"Verily, in the Remembrance of God Do Hearts Find Rest"

(Qur'an 13:28)

No pill, no distraction, no worldly success will bring the heart what prayer (remembrance of God) brings.

Remembrance is not just saying words.

It's pulling your heart back to its true home — back to the One who created it.

- Say, "Glory to God" (SubhanAllah) when you see something beautiful.
- Say, "Praise to God" (Alhamdulillah) when you survive a hard day.
- Say, "May God forgive me" (Astaghfirullah) when you feel broken inside.
- Say, "There is no might nor power except with God" when you feel too weak to move.

The heart does not find rest in forgetting pain.

The heart finds rest in remembering God *through* the pain.

Faith is not about feeling strong.

Faith is about holding on even when you feel weak.

And when you reach for God — even with the weakest, shaking hands — He catches you. Always.

Closing Reflection:

"You are not alone in your sadness.

You are not forgotten in your struggle.

You are not abandoned in your weakness.

Faith may flicker, but it does not die — because God never leaves His servant without a way back."

You are allowed to rest.
You are allowed to cry.
You are allowed to stay –
and rebuild at your own
pace.

CHAPTER 3

When You're the One Hurting

Voices from Survivors

Sometimes, the strongest voices are the quiet ones — the ones who have lived through the storm and stayed.

Here are real, anonymized reflections from survivors:

"I couldn't take the madness. I couldn't take the pain. I felt an overwhelming weight on me. I just wanted to disappear."

- (Anonymous survivor, age 56)

"I didn't want my life to end. I wanted the pain to end."

- (Anonymous survivor, age 28)

"It felt like drowning in a room full of air — everyone else breathing, but me suffocating."

- (Anonymous survivor, age 17)

"What saved me was the tiny, stubborn hope that maybe God could still change my story."

- (Anonymous survivor, age 35)

Each story is different. But one thing is always true:

Pain lies. It tells you there is no future — when in fact, God is still writing miracles you cannot see yet.

What Suicidal Thoughts Sound and Feel Like

Suicidal thoughts are not just thoughts of death.

They often sound like:

- *"I can't do this anymore."*
- *"Everyone would be better off without me."*
- *"I'm tired of hurting."*
- *"Nothing will ever change."*

And they often feel like:

- Heavy, crushing exhaustion
- Emotional numbness (not even sadness, just emptiness)
- Feeling invisible even when surrounded by people
- A strange, painful kind of calm — the mind trying to escape overwhelming pain

If you feel any of these things — you are not alone.

And more importantly:

You are not broken beyond repair.

Steps to Take in the Moment

When the pain is sharp — when you feel like giving up — you don't have to figure out everything. You just have to survive the next few minutes.

Here's how:

1. Ground Yourself Physically

- Feel your feet on the floor.

- Hold a cold object like a piece of ice.

- Name 5 things you can see, 4 things you can touch, 3 things you can hear, 2 things you can smell, 1 thing you can taste.

- Remind yourself: *I am here. I am real. This moment will pass.*

2. Turn to your Lord and Sustainer — Even If Your Voice Is Shaking

- Whisper "O Ever-Living, O Sustainer, by Your mercy I seek rescue."

- If you can't speak, just place your hand on your heart and think:

- *"God sees me. God hears me. God will not abandon me."*

3. Use Help Lines If you need a human voice:

- In the U.S.: 988 (Suicide and Crisis Lifeline — free and confidential)

The Power of a Village When You're Hurting

When despair creeps in, it tells you that you are alone — that no one would notice if you disappeared, that your pain is yours to carry alone.

But healing was never meant to be a solo journey.

Just as it takes a village to raise a child, it takes a village to hold a hurting soul.

We were created for connection: for shoulders to lean on, for arms to steady us when our knees buckle, for voices that whisper hope when our own voices fall silent.

A kind word, a simple meal shared, a listening ear — these are lifelines, not luxuries.

You are not a burden.

You are a heart worthy of being carried when it becomes too heavy to walk alone.

In faith, in family, in friendship — there is mercy waiting for you, woven through the village you deserve to belong to.

You were never meant to survive in isolation.

You were meant to heal together.

Reaching out is not weakness. It's wisdom.

God created community so we would not carry our burdens alone.

Calling in Your Village: You Don't Have to Fight Alone

In moments of emotional crisis, we often tell ourselves we should be able to handle things on our own. But healing was never meant to be a solo journey. Every one of us needs a "village" — a support system of trustworthy people who can stand by us, speak life into us, and step in when we are struggling to stand.

Think of your village as your emotional backup team — the people you can call, text, or lean on when the darkness feels too heavy. This isn't about being needy. This is about being *human*.

Here are the kinds of people you may want to intentionally include in your support village:

- A Therapist or Counselor

  Someone trained to help you process deep pain, trauma, anxiety, or suicidal thoughts. They are not just there for moments of crisis, but for building healthier thought patterns over time.

- A Doctor or Psychiatrist

  Mental health and physical health are deeply connected. A medical professional can rule out or treat underlying conditions (like thyroid imbalances or depression) and, if needed, help with medication support.

- A Trusted Friend or Family Member

  Choose someone who *listens without fixing*, respects your boundaries, and shows up with compassion. They don't need to have all the answers — they just need to be willing to walk with you.

- A Person of Faith or Spiritual Mentor

  Someone who can pray with you, remind you of your higher purpose, and speak hope when your soul feels weary. Whether it's your imam, a religious teacher, or a wise believer you trust, their presence can rekindle your connection with the Divine.

- A Crisis Support Contact

  This could be the 988 Lifeline or a local mental health helpline. Keep their number saved. Sometimes the safest voice is one you don't know personally — and that's okay.

You don't need to announce your pain to the world. But **you do need a few safe people you can call when you're sinking.**

Set up your village *before* the storm. Let them know they are part of your support team — and don't be afraid to say, "I need you right now."

Having backup doesn't make you weak. It makes you wise. Even the strongest souls need shoulders to lean on.

4. Journal or Voice Note Your Feelings

- Write what you feel without judgment.
- Cry out to God on paper or in a recording.
- Sometimes just releasing the words lightens the storm inside.

"It's Okay If All You Did Today Was Stay."

If you opened your eyes this morning,

If you breathed through one more heavy hour,

If you held on to your thread of life by trembling fingers — **you have already succeeded.**

Staying is an act of bravery.

You don't have to "feel good" to be doing well.

You just have to stay — and trust that with God, today's survival can lead to tomorrow's healing.

"So be patient. Indeed, the promise of God is true."
(Qur'an 30:60)

You are not alone.

You are not invisible.

You are not beyond mercy.

Stay.

Hope is being written for you even now.

Closing Reflection:

"Dear heart,
Today you stayed.
And that is enough.
God is nearer to you than your own heartbeat —
and His plans are kinder than your mind can imagine."

When the world feels
heavy, remember:
Allah's mercy is lighter
than your sorrow
and stronger than
your fears.

CHAPTER 4

Building Your Hope Plan

Opening Reflection: The Aftermath No One Prepares You For

- The silence after suicide is deafening.

- You're left holding not just grief, but *guilt, questions, shame,* and sometimes *anger.*

- "Could I have stopped it?" "Why didn't I see it?" "What do I say to others?"

"Say: Nothing will happen to us except what God has written for us."— **Surah At-Tawbah (9:51)**

The Questions That Haunt Survivors

- **How could I not have known?**

  - Most people who die by suicide *hide their pain.* They smile. They function. They keep going — until they don't. This is not your failure. This is their suffering.

- **Were there signs I missed?**

  o Sudden withdrawal or "goodbyes"

  o Giving away personal items

  o Mood swings or sudden peace after depression

  o Speaking vaguely about being tired, done, or at peace

- **What do I say to others?**

  o You are not obligated to explain details.

  o Say: "They were in pain. We're grieving and holding space for healing."

  o Say: "We ask for God's mercy, and your prayers for our family."

- **Can I pray for them?**

  o Yes — pray for *God's mercy*, for *forgiveness*, and for yourself.

  o The Prophet Mohammed (peace be upon him) said God forgives what He wills. You are not their Judge — you are their loved one.

Facing Shame, Judgement, and "What Will People Say?"

- Many families hide the truth out of fear.

- But silence breeds isolation, and secrecy worsens grief.

- You are allowed to grieve publicly and *truthfully*.

- Create safe space: place of worship (masjid, church, synagogue), therapists, or a private grief group.

"Indeed, with hardship comes ease."
— **Surah Ash-Sharh (94:6)**

What You Can Still Do for the One Who Died

- Make sincere prayer for them

- Give charity in their name

- Sponsor a water well

- Share good memories — not the ending

- Educate others to prevent future losses

"Whoever guides to something good will have a reward like the one who did it."

— **Muslim, 1893**

Support Tools for Families

- Join a grief support group (e.g., Faith-based bereavement circles, interfaith grief programs)

- Speak with clergy or grief counselor

- Talk to your children (age-appropriate truth)

- Avoid blaming language ("they were weak" or "they're in hell")

- Journal your grief. Start a "letter to them" journal.

Healing Is Not Forgetting — It's Living Again With Love

You don't "move on" from losing someone to suicide.

You move *with* it — slowly, with help, and with faith that God sees your ache and knows every tear. You are not alone. And neither are they.

The Aftermath No One Prepares You For

When someone you love dies by suicide, it doesn't feel like grief — it feels like a storm. A flood of questions. A silence that screams. A hundred "what ifs" that echo louder than condolences.

And if you're reading this chapter, you're likely one of those left behind.

Whether it was your parent, spouse, sibling, child, or friend — the pain is complicated. It's not just loss. It's confusion, guilt, even anger. It's shame in a society that doesn't know how to speak about suicide with compassion. It's trying to make peace with an ending that doesn't make sense.

"How Did I Not Know?"

This is often the first question survivors ask. But the truth is:

People in deep emotional pain often go silent before they go missing.

You may not have seen the signs.

You may have even spoken to them that very day.

Here's what survivors need to hear:

You are not at fault.

Even professionals sometimes miss the signs.

Common Signs (Sometimes Missed)

- Withdrawing from loved ones or responsibilities
- Talking vaguely about death or saying "I'm tired" or "You'd be better off without me"
- Sudden calmness after long sadness (a warning sign)
- Giving away personal possessions
- Loss of interest in previously loved things
- Increased use of drugs or alcohol
- Making "goodbye" gestures or closing accounts unexpectedly

But sometimes — there are **no signs at all**.

And that's one of the hardest truths families must live with.

What Do I Say to Others?

You may not know how to tell others. You may be afraid they'll judge your family or the person you lost. It's okay to keep it simple.

You can say:

"They were in pain. We are grieving and remembering their life with love."

"This loss was a result of deep suffering. Please pray for our peace and theirs."

You are not obligated to explain the details. What matters is that you're honest with your own grief.

Facing Shame, Judgment, and Silence

In many cultures and faith communities — including among Muslims and Christians— suicide is stigmatized. People may ask hurtful questions or make ignorant comments. Some may suggest your loved one "gave up on God" or "chose hell."

Here's what I want you to know:

- Your grief is valid.

- Your love for them doesn't end here.

- Their pain was real — but so is your healing.

Suicide is not the story of their soul. It is a chapter — not their conclusion.

Can I Still Help Them?

Yes.

Whether through prayer, charity, or acts of kindness in their name — you can continue to honor them.

Support for You, Too

You don't have to heal alone. Seek out:

- Grief counseling (general or faith-based)
- Support groups (in-person or online)
- Trusted community members
- Therapists who specialize in traumatic loss

And most importantly — give yourself time. There is no right timeline for grief.

Online Support Groups for Suicide Loss Survivors

1. Alliance of Hope

A 24/7 online forum dedicated to suicide loss survivors, offering peer support, resources, and a compassionate community. Ideal for those seeking connection at any hour.

2. American Foundation for Suicide Prevention (AFSP)

AFSP provides a comprehensive directory of support groups across the U.S., including virtual options. Their Healing Conversations program connects new survivors with trained volunteers for one-on-one support.

3. Survivors of Suicide (SOS) – Eluna Network

Provides a locator tool to find both in-person and online support groups tailored for suicide loss survivors. They also offer resources for supporting children and teens after a suicide death.

4. 988 Suicide & Crisis Lifeline

Dial or Text 988 for Immediate, Confidential Support

The **988 Suicide & Crisis Lifeline** offers **free, confidential emotional support 24 hours a day, 7 days a week** across the United States. It connects people in suicidal crisis or emotional distress with trained crisis counselors through a network of over 200 local crisis centers, blending local care with national standards.

Whether you **call, text, or chat**, you'll receive **judgment-free support**. If speaking feels intimidating, texting is also an option. The Lifeline is here to meet you where you are—with compassion, respect, and no pressure.

What to Expect When You Call 988:

1. You'll hear a brief message with options for specialized services (including Spanish-language, LGBTQI+ support, Veterans support, or local connections).

2. You may hear hold music as you're routed to an available counselor.

3. A trained counselor will greet you and introduce themselves.

4. They'll ask about your safety and emotional state.

5. From there, they'll listen deeply, help you process your situation, offer support, and connect you to any needed resources.

Calls typically last around 10 minutes, but they can be shorter or extend up to 25 to 45 minutes, depending on your needs. There's no time limit—you are the priority.

Reaching out may feel scary, but connecting with someone can save your life. You don't have to go through this alone. The 988 Lifeline exists to support you, without judgment, whenever you need help the most.

Real-Life Testimonies

Sarah's Story (Sibling)

"My older brother Adam was the most outgoing person you'd ever meet. He was always cracking jokes, planning camping trips, and sending good morning texts to our family group chat. The day before he died, he called to check on me and talked about how excited he was to help me move into my new apartment.

When I got the call the next morning, I thought it was a mistake. I remember shouting, 'No, he was just laughing yesterday!'

I went through every conversation we ever had, trying to find something — anything — that would've told me he was in that much pain. But there was nothing. No notes. No warning. Nothing but a deep, invisible sadness he never let us see.

That's what makes this kind of loss so brutal. You're left loving someone you didn't know was suffering. And now I tell everyone: just because someone seems okay doesn't mean they are. Ask twice. Ask again. And if you feel something is off, follow that feeling."

A Mother's Story

"When my daughter Layla took her life at 22, I felt like my heart was ripped out of my chest. She was in college, studying psychology. She had friends, she was smart, funny, and deeply spiritual. There was no note. No warning. Just this unbearable silence.

People asked me, 'Didn't you know something was wrong?' And the truth is, I didn't. She smiled all the time. She texted me the night before to say, 'I love you, Mama.' That was the last message I got.

I now know how much she must have been hiding. And I don't carry shame anymore — just love, and a commitment to speak out so other mothers won't feel alone."

A Spouse's Story

"My wife battled depression silently for years. I thought I was helping. I tried to cheer her up, tell her to pray more, think positively. I thought if we just kept moving forward, she'd get better.

The day I found her, everything changed. I still struggle to breathe some days. I replay our last moments constantly. But what hurts most is not knowing how much she was holding in, just to keep me from worrying. Now I tell everyone: listen with more than your ears. See with more than your eyes. And love without assumptions."

A Teen's Story

"When my dad died, everyone just kept telling me to 'be strong for your mom.' I was 16. I didn't know how to grieve. I didn't know if I was allowed to talk about the fact that it was suicide. I felt so confused, so angry, and honestly... ashamed.

What helped me was writing letters to him in a journal. I still do it sometimes. And I found a teen grief group online where we talk openly. I wish he had known how much we needed him. But now I just try to be someone others can talk to — without judgment."

A Child's Reflection

"I was nine when my older cousin died. I didn't really understand what suicide meant. I just knew everyone was crying, and I wasn't allowed to ask questions. I remember thinking: did she stop loving us?

Now that I'm older, I know it wasn't about love. She must have been hurting in ways we couldn't see. And I think we should talk about that, not hide it."

Reflection to Carry With You

"Even if you didn't get to say goodbye... Even if you didn't know they were hurting... Even if your heart is broken — you are still here. And your life still has meaning."

Healing doesn't erase your scars. It teaches you to wear them as signs of your unseen victories.

CHAPTER 5

The Many Faces of Despair

∞

Despair Wears Many Faces

Despair does not always look like sadness on the outside.

It does not have one story, one age, one language, or one face.

It can come from:

- A shattered marriage.

- A heavy illness diagnosis.

- The silence after trauma.

- The crushing shame of a public mistake.

- The invisible exhaustion of giving more than you have left to give.

Despair is universal.

The ache may have different names, but the heartache is the same.

Divorce, Abuse, Financial Loss, Illness, Trauma, Shame

Divorce

- Feeling unwanted, rejected, discarded.
- Losing not just a spouse, but dreams, routines, even identity.

Abuse

- Carrying invisible wounds on your heart and body.
- Wondering if love will ever mean safety again.

Financial Loss

- Feeling like a failure.
- Crushing worry over survival.
- Shame about not being "successful enough."

Chronic Illness

- Living in a body that feels like an enemy.
- Mourning the life you once had.

Trauma

- Flashbacks that rip you out of the present.
- Trust issues that isolate you from the world.

Shame

- Believing you are broken, beyond repair, unworthy of love or forgiveness.

Each wound is different.

But the ache?

The ache is something only God fully sees.

"Indeed, God is ever Seeing of His servants."
(Qur'an 40:44)

Common Reasons People Die by Suicide

1. Veterans and First Responders

- **Cause**: PTSD, survivor's guilt, moral injury, chronic pain, isolation after service.

- **Insight**: Many feel abandoned after years of service; haunted by what they've seen or done.

- **Example phrase**: *"They survived war zones, but couldn't survive the silence that followed."*

2. The Elderly

- **Cause**: Loneliness, loss of independence, chronic illness, death of spouse or friends.

- **Insight**: They often feel invisible, forgotten, or like a burden.

- **Faith link**: *"Even in old age, your Lord has not left you."*

3. Terminal Illness / Chronic Pain

- **Cause**: Debilitating physical suffering, fear of being a burden, loss of quality of life.

- **Insight**: Sometimes people just want the pain to stop, not life itself.

- **Faith link**: Reminders of reward for patience and that every second of hardship is recorded.

4. Divorce and Relationship Loss

- **Cause**: Rejection, loneliness, identity crisis, shame, loss of future dreams.

- **Insight**: Especially true in cultures where marriage is deeply tied to status or self-worth.

- **Faith link**: "God is close to the brokenhearted" (Qur'an 2:286, 94:6)

5. Financial Ruin or Disaster (fire, eviction, job loss)

- **Cause**: Hopelessness, shame, feeling like they've failed as a provider.

- **Insight**: Men in particular often suffer in silence under the weight of expectations.

- **Faith link**: *"And whoever relies on God – He is sufficient for him."* **(Qur'an 65:3)**

6. Grief: Death of a Loved One

- **Cause**: Intense loss, especially when the deceased was a spouse, child, or parent.

- **Insight**: Many feel "what is the point of living anymore?"

- **Faith link**: The Prophet Muhammad (peace be upon him) wept for his son Ibrahim and still reminded us of patience in loss.

7. Mental Illness

- **Cause**: Depression, bipolar disorder, schizophrenia, borderline personality, etc.

- **Insight**: Many don't *want* to die — they want to escape their mind.

- **Faith link**: Reminders that illness (even of the mind) is not a sin, and God knows our struggle.

8. Trauma or Abuse

- **Cause**: Childhood sexual abuse, domestic violence, assault.

- **Insight**: Victims often internalize shame and pain that makes them feel "damaged."

- **Faith link**: "Indeed, God is with those who endure patiently." **(Qur'an 2:153)**

9. Sudden Public Shame / Scandal

- **Cause**: Reputation loss, public humiliation, online bullying.

- **Insight**: The desire to escape the gaze and judgment of others.

- **Faith link**: *"If the world turns its back on you, God never does."*

10. Existential Emptiness / Spiritual Crisis

- **Cause**: Loss of purpose, disconnection from faith or meaning.

- **Insight**: Often hidden behind smiles — but deeply rooted in feeling "lost."

- **Faith link**: "Verily, in the remembrance of God do hearts find rest." **(Qur'an 13:28)**

Real Solutions by Category

1. Veterans & First Responders

Why They Struggle: PTSD, survivor's guilt, chronic pain, loss of identity after service

Solutions:

- Trauma-informed therapy (EMDR, CBT)

- Veterans Crisis Line (988, then press 1)

- Faith-based chaplain support

- Men's groups or retreats for healing the masculine wound

- Islamic reminder: *"Do not kill yourselves. Surely God is Most Merciful to you."* **(Qur'an 4:29)**

2. Elderly

Why They Struggle: Loneliness, loss of purpose, bereavement

Solutions:

- Senior companionship programs

- Faith-based senior circles

- Grief counseling

- Mobile prayer

- Islamic reminder: *"And your Lord has decreed...kindness to parents."* **(Qur'an 17:23)**

3. Chronic Illness / Terminal Diagnosis

Why They Struggle: Pain, hopelessness, feeling like a burden

Solutions:

- Palliative care / pain management

- Mental health support in oncology units

- Spiritual chaplaincy

- Family counseling

- **Reminder of reward for patience**: *"Those who patiently persevere will receive their reward without measure."* **(Qur'an 39:10)**

4. Divorce / Relationship Loss

Why They Struggle: Shame, heartbreak, shattered identity

Solutions:

- Support groups for divorced women/men

- Grief and identity-based therapy

- Community reintegration programs

- Marriage healing retreats (for second chances)

- Faith link: *"Perhaps you hate a thing and God makes therein much good."* **(Qur'an 4:19)**

5. Financial Loss / Fire / Tragedy

Why They Struggle: Helplessness, shame, loss of status

Solutions:

- Charity funds

- Crisis intervention grants

- Job skills & emotional recovery programs

- Shelter and spiritual counseling from faith-based networks

- *"And We will surely test you with loss... but give good tidings to the patient."* **(Qur'an 2:155)**

6. Death of a Loved One

Why They Struggle: Loss of emotional anchor, despair

Solutions:

- Grief counseling

- Bereavement groups

- Spiritual journaling

- "Letters to the lost" healing activity

- *"Every soul shall taste death... and to God you will be returned."* **(Qur'an 3:185)**

7. Mental Illness (Depression, Bipolar, Anxiety)

Why They Struggle: Persistent darkness, mood swings, shame

Solutions:

- Licensed therapists

- Medication and faith-based therapy

- Prayer and structured routine of worship + mental health plan

- *"Indeed, with hardship comes ease."* **(Qur'an 94:6)**

8. Trauma / Abuse Survivors

Why They Struggle: Shame, isolation, unresolved pain

Solutions:

- Trauma-informed therapy (especially for sexual trauma)
- Safe shelters (for women escaping abuse)
- Support groups for survivors
- Faith-based abuse prevention education
- *"And God is the best of Protectors."* **(Qur'an 12:64)**

9. Public Shame / Cancel Culture / Scandal

Why They Struggle: Loss of reputation, humiliation, cyberbullying

Solutions:

- Reputation repair counseling
- Online mental health crisis lines
- Digital detox and faith-based rebuilding circles
- *"And He is the One who accepts repentance from His servants and pardons misdeeds."* **(Qur'an 42:25)**

10. Spiritual Crisis / No Belief in Anything

Why They Struggle: Existential dread, lack of meaning

Solutions:

- Interfaith suicide prevention lines

- Mindfulness and nature-based healing retreats

- Gentle call to worshipping the Creator through emotional support

- *"Verily, in the remembrance of God do hearts find rest."* **(Qur'an 13:28)**

Veterans and the Weight of War

Many veterans return from service carrying invisible wounds. These aren't just physical injuries — they are psychological, emotional, and spiritual. After facing war, death, or traumatic events, the "normal" world can feel unbearable.

Why Suicide Rates Are High Among Veterans:

- **PTSD (Post-Traumatic Stress Disorder)**: Nightmares, flashbacks, emotional numbness.

- **Moral Injury**: Guilt over actions during war that clash with personal or spiritual values.

- **Isolation**: Difficulty reintegrating into civilian life, feeling like no one understands.

- **Chronic Pain & Disability**: Long-term physical suffering from injuries.

- **Loss of Purpose**: After years of structure, discipline, and "mission," civilian life feels directionless.

Trauma-Informed Therapy for Veterans

"Trauma-informed" means the therapist understands the depth and layers of trauma — and doesn't re-trigger it during treatment.

Effective Approaches:

1. **EMDR (Eye Movement Desensitization and Reprocessing)**

   - Helps rewire how the brain stores traumatic memories.

   - Proven to help veterans overcome PTSD flashbacks.

2. **CBT (Cognitive Behavioral Therapy)**

   - Focuses on breaking destructive thought patterns.

   - Helps veterans reframe guilt, self-blame, and hopelessness.

3. **Somatic Therapy**

   - Helps process trauma that lives in the body (common for soldiers).

   - Uses breathwork, movement, and awareness to release stored pain.

4. **Faith-Based Counseling**

   - For veterans with a spiritual background, integrating prayer, and trust in God can deeply aid healing.

5. Group Therapy

- Sharing stories with other veterans can reduce isolation and offer brotherhood in healing.

Muslims who are veterans may find comfort in knowing that they are not weak for needing help. The Prophet Muhammad (peace be upon him) wept, grieved, and sought solitude — yet never hid his emotion. Emotional honesty is not weakness — it is *courage*.

"Dear Veteran: You Survived War. You Deserve Peace."

You do not need to suffer alone. There are therapies built for what you've been through. You are not broken — your nervous system has simply been in survival mode for too long. Healing is possible. Mercy is real. And the strength you showed in war can be used again — to reclaim your peace.

A Letter from the Chaplain

Dear Veteran,

I know you've seen things that most people will never understand.

You've carried weight that doesn't fit into words — memories, loss, maybe regret. You've served your country with honor, but now the silence of coming home feels louder than the battlefield ever did. And maybe, just maybe, you've started to wonder if your life still has purpose... if the pain will ever lift.

But I want you to hear me clearly:

You matter. You are not alone. And your story is not over.

Pain is not a sign of weakness. Even the Prophet Muhammad (peace be upon him) cried. He grieved. He felt alone. But he always turned back to the One who never leaves — **God**, the Most Merciful.

Your survival is not an accident. It's a sign.

You were not kept alive to suffer — you were kept alive to *heal*, to *grow*, and to be a living sign that redemption is real.

The things you did, the things you saw — they don't define your soul. God sees your heart. And where people might judge, He forgives.

So if you're tired, come back to peace.

If you're angry, come back to prayer.

If you're drowning, call out — even if it's just a whisper.

We are here.

The line is open.

The mercy is near.

With compassion and hope,

Suicide Methods Among Females (U.S. 2022–2023)

- **Poisoning (including drug overdoses)** is the most common method among girls and women.

- (Especially overdoses involving prescription medications, opioids, and over-the-counter drugs.)

- **Suffocation (including hanging)** is the second most common method among females.

- (This has sadly increased in recent years among teenage girls.)

- **Firearms** are less common among females compared to males, but firearm-related suicides among women have also been rising over the past few years.

Key Insights:

- Females are more likely to attempt suicide than males, but they often use methods that allow for a possibility of rescue (like poisoning).

- Males die by suicide at much higher rates because they tend to use more immediately lethal methods like firearms.

(Source: CDC Vital Statistics Reports 2022–2023 and American Foundation for Suicide Prevention)

Reasons Men Over 75 Are at Higher Risk for Suicide:

6. **Social Isolation and Loneliness**

   - Older men are more likely to live alone after the death of a spouse or friends.

   - They often experience decreased social connection, which is a huge risk factor for depression and suicidal thoughts.

7. **Chronic Illness and Pain**

   - Many elderly men face serious medical issues like cancer, heart disease, arthritis, and chronic pain.

   - Physical suffering without hope for recovery can lead to feelings of despair.

8. **Loss of Purpose or Identity**

   - After retirement, many men feel they have lost their role as providers, protectors, and leaders.

   - Without a strong sense of ongoing purpose, life may feel meaningless.

9. **Unrecognized Depression**

   - Depression in older men is often underdiagnosed and undertreated.

   - They might not recognize or admit they are struggling emotionally, seeing it as a weakness.

10. Access to Lethal Means

- Older men often have easier access to firearms and are more likely to use them, leading to more fatal suicide attempts.

11. Cultural Factors ("Be Tough" Mentality)

- Older generations of men were raised with the idea that seeking help is weak.

- They are less likely to seek counseling, psychiatric care, or even talk openly about emotional pain.

12. Grief and Loss

- Loss of a spouse, children, siblings, or close friends can compound feelings of deep sadness and loneliness.

- Some may also experience "survivor's guilt" if many loved ones have passed away.

How Faith Can Help:

- Reminding elderly men of their continuing value. In Islam, being an elder is honored.

- Teaching that suffering is purification.

- Emphasizing that patience brings reward, and that every hardship expiates sins.

- Offering community connection (visiting the elderly, involving them in faith-based communities)

Why Are Elderly Men at Higher Risk of Suicide?

As men grow older, many face hidden struggles that can weigh heavily on the heart.

The loss of loved ones, chronic pain, loneliness, and the feeling that they are no longer needed can lead to deep sadness. Often, older men were raised to "be strong" and hide their emotions, making it even harder for them to ask for help.

Sadly, depression is often missed or untreated in elderly men. Some may lose their sense of purpose after retirement. Others may suffer quietly through illnesses or grief, believing they must endure alone.

In truth, every life remains precious to God — especially those who have lived long and faced many tests. Islam honors the elderly. Their prayers are powerful. Their patience is deeply rewarded.

The Prophet Mohammed (peace be upon him) said:

"No fatigue, nor disease, nor sorrow, nor sadness, nor hurt, nor distress befalls a Muslim — even if it were the prick he receives from a thorn — but that God expiates some of his sins for it."

(Sahih al-Bukhari 5641)

Struggles in old age are not a burden without meaning — they are opportunities for forgiveness, mercy, and elevation in the Hereafter.

In our families and communities, we must cherish our elders, listen to them, visit them, and remind them that they are not forgotten.

Reflection and Prayer for Elderly Men Feeling Sad:

"O God, You are the Light of the heavens and the earth. Bring light to my heart when it feels heavy, and hope to my soul when it feels weary. Make my days filled with gratitude and my nights filled with patience. And when the time comes, let me return to You in peace, forgiven and honored among the righteous. Ameen."

How Families Can Support Elderly Men at Risk

1. Stay Connected:

Visit them regularly. A simple conversation can brighten their entire week.

2. Ask About Their Feelings:

Gently ask how they are coping. Listen without judgment. Even strong men need to be heard.

3. Encourage Purpose:

Help them find new activities: teaching grandchildren, volunteering at their place of worship, gardening, writing memoirs. Purpose gives life new meaning.

4. Watch for Signs of Depression:

Notice if they withdraw, talk about feeling useless, lose interest in things, or mention death. Don't ignore subtle cries for help.

5. Respect Their Dignity:

Offer help respectfully. No one wants to feel like a burden. Small acts of support (help with errands, health appointments) go a long way.

6. Remind Them of God's Mercy:

Share scripture about God's kindness, reward for patience, and how every hardship erases sins.

7. Get Professional Help When Needed:

If depression or hopelessness seems severe, gently encourage medical help or counseling. Islamic therapists are becoming more available.

Closing Reminder:

Our elders are treasures — not to be forgotten, but to be cherished and honored. Their prayers are a protection for the entire family.

How Different People Carry the Same Ache

Despair speaks many languages:

- Tears behind closed doors.

- Angry outbursts.

- Silent withdrawal.

- Exhaustion that never leaves.

The pain looks different, but the longing is the same:

"Please, someone see me. Please, someone tell me I matter."

And God says:

"And We are nearer to him than [his] jugular vein." (Qur'an 50:16)

God sees.

God knows.

God understands every hidden wound.

Chart: "What You're Facing + Where You Can Turn"

Struggle	Reminders / Where to Turn
Divorce or Heartbreak	Healing is real. Prayer, therapy, trusted community.
Abuse Survivor	You are not to blame. Trauma counseling, faith-based therapy, protective communities.
Financial Loss	Provision comes after loss. Islamic charities, community charity programs, budgeting support.
Illness or Chronic Pain	Every pain erases sins. Medical care, support groups, prayers for cure.
Depression, Anxiety, Trauma	Your brokenness is not your fault. Counseling, prayer, crisis support lines.
Elderly Isolation	God never leaves you. Spiritual companionship, faith-based community, family reconnection.
Youth Struggles	God chose you for this time for a reason. Counseling, youth groups, mentorship programs.
Caregiver Burnout	God rewards the unseen burdens. Support networks, respite care, personal worship even in small moments.

Closing Reflection

"No matter how despair wraps itself around your heart, you are never outside the reach of God's mercy.

The same Lord who split the sea for Moses (Musa) can split the darkness in your life — and bring you into the light again."

Survival is not weakness.

It is worship in its rawest, most beautiful form.

CHAPTER 6

What the Mind Believes, the Body Feels

———————∞———————

The mind and the body are not separate worlds.

What we carry in our hearts and minds eventually shows up in our bodies — often as exhaustion, pain, or illness.

Depression can cause:

- Extreme tiredness (even after sleeping)
- Loss of appetite or overeating
- Headaches, muscle aches, and back pain
- Weak immune response (getting sick more often)

Anxiety can cause:

- Racing heartbeat and chest tightness
- Sweating, trembling
- Stomach problems like nausea or diarrhea
- Chronic tension and migraines

Trauma can cause:

- Sleep disorders
- Body pain without clear medical explanation
- Hypervigilance (constantly feeling unsafe)
- Hormonal and immune system damage over time

Pain that is not processed emotionally often becomes pain the body tries to express physically.

"Indeed, in the remembrance of God do hearts find rest."

(Qur'an 13:28)

When the heart rests, the body often follows.

The Body's Cry for Relief: Insomnia, Numbness, Self-Harm

Sometimes the body doesn't whisper — it screams.

Insomnia:

- Racing thoughts won't let you rest.
- Anxiety about tomorrow feels unbearable.
- The heart pounds even when the room is quiet.

Numbness:

- Feeling disconnected from your own emotions.
- Going through the motions of life without truly feeling alive.

Self-Harm:

- Trying to turn invisible emotional pain into visible physical pain.
- Hoping that hurting the body will somehow release the storm inside.

Self-harm is not weakness or attention-seeking.

It's an unspoken cry: *"Please, help me find another way to survive."*

Spiritual Depression vs. Clinical Depression

It's important to understand the difference — because misdiagnosis can cause more harm.

Spiritual Depression:

- Feeling distant from God.

- Losing motivation for prayer.

- Feeling guilty, disconnected, empty inside.

Clinical Depression:

- Persistent sadness or numbness most of the day, nearly every day.

- Physical symptoms (like sleep problems, appetite changes, physical pain).

- Inability to function in daily life (work, school, relationships).

You can have one, the other, or both at the same time.

If you feel spiritually lost, return gently to God through prayer and reading Qur'an.

If you feel clinically depressed, also seek medical and psychological help.

Faith and healing are not opposites.

Faith and healing walk hand in hand.

When to Seek Therapy, Medication, or Both — and How Islam Supports Healing

Seek professional therapy if:

- You feel hopeless most days for more than two weeks.

- You have thoughts of harming yourself.

- You struggle to function in normal daily activities.

- Your sleep, appetite, or energy levels are severely affected.

Consider medication if:

- Therapy alone isn't enough to stabilize your symptoms.

- You suffer from severe depression, anxiety, PTSD, or mood disorders that impair your ability to live daily life.

- A trusted, knowledgeable doctor recommends it.

Islam Supports Seeking Healing

The Prophet Muhammad (peace be upon him) said:

"Make use of medical treatment, for God has not made a disease without appointing a remedy for it."
(Sahih al-Bukhari 5678)

You do not have to suffer in silence.

Islam invites us to seek healing — through prayer, through medicine, through therapy, through community.

Faith does not mean pretending you're okay when you're not.

Faith means trusting that healing is possible — and taking the steps God has placed in front of you.

Therapy is not a lack of trust in God.

Medication is not a lack of patience.

Seeking help is not weakness. It's courage.

You are not "less" because you hurt.

You are a human — and God is the Most Merciful, who created healing for every pain.

Closing Reflection:

"Your heart was never meant to carry everything alone.

Your mind was never meant to heal itself without help.

Reach for healing — and trust that God has already written your restoration."

Even in the darkest ocean,
a heart tied to hope
will always find
its way back to the shore.

CHAPTER 7

Creating a Life Worth Staying For

Healing Is Built, One Gentle Step at a Time

You don't have to create a perfect life.

You just need to build a life with enough light to walk through the darkness.

A life with enough hope to hold onto — even on hard days.

Hope doesn't happen by accident.

Hope is built.

Hope is planted.

Hope is nurtured.

And you are worthy of that rebuilding.

Building Micro-Joys, Prayer Routines, and Self-Compassion

1. Building Micro-Joys

- **Micro-joys** are tiny moments that spark comfort, beauty, or gratitude.
- Examples:

- o A warm cup of tea.

- o Watching birds fly overhead.

- o Smelling a favorite scent.

- o Finishing one small task.

Practice:

Every day, write down one small thing that made you smile, even for a second.

2. Building Prayer Routines

- Even if your heart feels heavy, return to simple, small acts of worship.

- Examples:

  - o Pray asking God to open your heart.

  - o Whisper "Astaghfirullah (God forgive me)" when feeling overwhelmed.

  - o Read one verse of Qur'an a day — not for obligation, but for oxygen.

3. Practicing Self-Compassion

- Stop measuring yourself by productivity.

- Talk to yourself as you would a beloved friend:

  - o *"You're doing your best."*

  - o *"God sees your effort."*

  - o *"Today was hard, but you stayed."*

Practice:

Each evening, write yourself a gentle note thanking yourself for something you did — even if it was just breathing through the day.

Making Room for Hope Again

Hope feels scary after you've been hurt.

It feels dangerous to believe good things could happen.

But God says:

"And whoever relies upon God — then He is sufficient for him."

(Qur'an 65:3)

Hope is not naïve.

Hope is a muscle   and you can rebuild it.

Start small:

Hope for one peaceful moment today.

Hope for one tiny mercy tomorrow.

Hope that God is already arranging something better for you — even if you can't see it yet.

Finding Safe People and Safe Spaces

Healing requires safety.

You cannot heal while constantly feeling threatened or judged.

Find Safe People:

- Those who listen more than they lecture.
- Those who remind you of God with kindness, not fear.
- Those who accept you in your messy healing, not just your polished moments.

Find Safe Spaces:

- A quiet corner of the masjid or place of worship.
- A park bench under open sky.
- An online group of compassionate believers.
- A therapist who honors your faith and humanity.

Prayer for Reconnection and Rebuilding

Here is a simple, powerful prayer you can whisper in moments of doubt:

"O God, return my heart to You in a beautiful return.

Heal what is broken within me.

Plant hope where despair has lived.

Build for me a life filled with light, love, and remembrance of You.

Ameen."

Closing Reflection:

"You are allowed to rebuild.

You are allowed to hope again.

You are allowed to create a life worth living —

And God, the Most Merciful, will help you wtih every small step you take toward healing."

You stayed.
And somewhere,
unseen by you,
angels wrote it down
as a victory
in your book of life.

CHAPTER 8

You Were Never Alone

Reflections on God's Closeness in Despair

There were moments when you thought no one saw you crying into the pillow.

No one noticed the prayers whispered between sobs.

No one cared about the ache you carried in silence.

But God was there. Always.

"When My servants ask you concerning Me — indeed I am near. I respond to the call of the supplicant when he calls upon Me."

(Qur'an 2:186)

Even when your prayer felt dry.

Even when you couldn't find the words.

Even when you felt unworthy to ask.

God was closer than your own heartbeat.

He heard.

He knew.

He carried you through nights you didn't think you would survive.

Your survival itself is a sign:

He never left you.

Global Lesson: The Power of Community

Across the world, one of the strongest shields against suicide is belonging.

When people feel connected — to family, faith, friends, or community — they are far less likely to lose hope, even when facing hardship.

In Barbados, a country with one of the lowest suicide rates, strong family ties and a deeply rooted faith culture protect people from the loneliness and despair that fuel suicide in other parts of the world.

In contrast, places like Lesotho which has the highest suicide rate, where poverty, illness, and isolation are overwhelming, show us how dangerous it is when people suffer alone, unseen.

Connection saves lives.

Isolation endangers them.

As individuals, as families, and as communities, we must rebuild bonds of care, faith, and compassion — because one warm hand, one kind word, one invitation to be seen can make the difference between despair and hope.

Islam teaches us:

"The believers are like one body; if one part hurts, the whole body responds with sleeplessness and fever."
(Sahih al-Bukhari and Muslim)

In every society, and especially in ours, strengthening the ties between hearts is not just good — it is lifesaving.

When the weight feels heavy, whisper back to your heart:

"I am held by God."

Hardships pass.

Wounds heal.

Patience is never lost. It is stored with God — and it will be returned to you, more beautiful than you can imagine.

Hold on. Hope is near.

How to Support Others

Sometimes we are not the ones struggling — we are standing beside someone who is.

How to support someone facing despair:

- Listen without judgment.

- Offer presence, not lectures.

- Say "I'm here" more than "You should..."

- Remind them gently: *"God's mercy is bigger than this moment."*

- Help them connect to professional help if needed — *and* offer spiritual encouragement.

Remember:

You don't have to fix them.

You just have to love them.

God is the true Healer.

Letting Go of Control (For Caregivers and Family)

When someone you love is struggling, your instinct is to fix it, to save them.

But real love understands:

- You cannot heal someone else's wounds.

- You cannot force their recovery.

- You cannot control their journey.

You can pray.

You can offer your hand.

You can walk beside them.

But the heart is in the Hands of God — not ours.

"And know that God intervenes between a man and his heart."

(Qur'an 8:24)

For caregivers and family:

- Set boundaries when needed (to protect your own health).

- Get your own support (therapy, groups, spiritual guidance).

- Focus on being an anchor, not the ocean.

Healing takes time. And it is written by God's perfect wisdom — not our frantic efforts.

Faith, Relapse, Recovery, and the Long Road Ahead

Recovery is not a straight line.

There will be relapses.

There will be days you fall back into sadness, anxiety, despair.

But relapse is not failure.

It's part of the process of strengthening, healing, and growing.

Faith may rise and fall — but God's mercy never shrinks.

- If you fall, stand up again.
- If you fall again, crawl if you must — but stay facing God.
- Know that every step you take toward healing is seen, counted, and rewarded.

Healing is a long road.

Some days will feel like victory.

Some days will feel like starting over.

Both days are valid. Both days are sacred.

The long road is still the right road.

Resources List: Where to Turn for Help

Suicide Crisis Hotlines:

- **United States:** 988 Suicide & Crisis Lifeline
- **United Kingdom:** Samaritans (116 123)
- **Canada:** Talk Suicide Canada (1-833-456-4566)

Closing Reflection

"Even when your hands were too tired to reach up,

God's mercy was still reaching down.

Even when your heart doubted, God still believed in the beauty written inside you.

You were never walking alone.

And you never will be."

Farewell Message to the Reader

∞

Dear Heart,

If you are reading these final pages, it means you stayed.

You breathed through the hard moments.

You allowed light to find you again, even if it was only a single, trembling ray.

Please know this:

You are not broken beyond repair.

You are not invisible to the One who created you.

You are not walking alone, no matter how long the road may feel.

Healing is not about reaching perfection.

Healing is about choosing hope — even when you are tired, even when you are afraid.

It is about trusting that every tear, every whispered prayer, every small step toward life matters.

God sees you.

God is near.

And God is not done writing your story.

Stay. Hope. Trust. Heal.

May God flood your heart with light, surround you with love, and grant you peace in both this life and the Next.

Ameen.

With gentleness and prayers,

Halimah Jordan

Author of Faith as a Lifeline

Appendix

∞

Appendix A: Bonus Tools for Daily Healing

Daily Gratitude Prompts:

(Use a journal or a simple notebook.)

- Today, I smiled when I saw/heard/felt _____.
- One thing I survived today (even if small) was _____.
- I thank God today for _____.
- One way God showed me mercy today was _____.
- I am proud of myself today because _____.

Self-Compassion Reminders:

- Healing is not linear. It's okay to have bad days.
- My value is not based on how much I accomplish today.
- Small steps are still steps.
- God sees the battles I fight silently.

Emergency Calm-Down Tools:

- Take five deep breaths, in through the nose, out through the mouth.

- Place a hand on your heart and whisper, "God is with me."

- Touch something cold (ice cube, cool cloth) to ground yourself.

- Walk outside and notice five beautiful things God has created.

Appendix B: The Hope Contract

1. The Hope Contract

Template Text for Readers:

I, _____,

Commit to remembering that despair is not the end of my story.

I promise to reach out for help if my sadness grows heavy.

I promise to remind myself that God's mercy is greater than any darkness I face.

If I feel overwhelmed, I will contact: _____ (trusted person / helpline)

I believe that my life, even in struggle, holds meaning beyond what I can see today.*

Signed: _____

Date: _____

Fill out this contract and keep it somewhere visible (phone, mirror, journal).

Appendix C: 7 Days of Heart Healing

Day	Focus	Affirmation
Day 1	Hope Still Lives	"Hope is still alive in me, even if it feels small."
Day 2	Breath of Mercy	"Mercy fills every breath I take."
Day 3	Small Gratitude	"Gratitude is growing in my heart, one small seed at a time."
Day 4	Release the Heavy	"I release what I cannot carry — and trust I am supported."
Day 5	Anchor Prayer	"I am sustained by divine strength, even when I feel weak."
Day 6	Mercy in Mistakes	"My mistakes do not erase my worth or my future."
Day 7	Plant a Seed	"Every small step I take matters. I am moving toward healing."

Appendix D: Crisis Calm Kit

Emergency Calm Actions:

Ground Your Body:

- Feel your feet firmly on the ground.

- Press your hands together and focus on the feeling.

- Look around and name:

    o 5 things you can see

    o 4 things you can touch

    o 3 things you can hear

    o 2 things you can smell

    o 1 thing you can taste

Use Cooling or Soothing Touch:

- Hold an ice cube or a cool cloth.

- Let yourself feel the sensation fully — this reminds your brain you are still here, still alive, still breathing.

Deep Breathing:

- Inhale slowly for 4 counts.

- Hold for 4 counts.

- Exhale slowly for 6 counts.

- Repeat 3–5 times until your heart rate slows.

Anchor Yourself with Words:

Choose a simple calming phrase and repeat it gently in your mind or whisper it:

"I am safe right now."

"This moment will pass."

"I am not alone in my pain."

"Hope is still alive in me."

"I am loved more than I know."

Hold a Symbol of Comfort:

- A favorite book, a comforting photo — something that reminds you of safety, meaning, or hope.

Emergency Spirit-Lifting Prompts:

If You Are Spiritually Inclined:

- Whisper a short prayer, mantra, or reminder like:
    - "God, be near to me now."
    - "Source of Mercy, help me find light again."
    - "I am in Your hands."

If You Are Non-Religious:

- Repeat gentle affirmations like:
    - "I am still breathing. I am still fighting."
    - "There is more to my story than this moment."

If You Can:

- Step outside into nature.

- Feel the sun, the breeze, the earth beneath you.

- Remind yourself: "I am part of something larger than this pain."

Quick Note:

This is not the end of your story.

Pain lies to you — but your survival is the truth.

Even the smallest act of staying — breathing, sitting, grounding — is an act of immense courage.

Hold on.

The storm is not the end.

Mercy, healing, and new beginnings still wait for you.

Emergency Actions:

- Touch something cold (ice cube, cold water).

- Ground yourself: Name 5 things you see, 4 you hear, 3 you feel, 2 you smell, 1 you taste.

- Hold a Quran, even if you don't read it — touch mercy physically.

Emergency Prayer:

"O Turner of the hearts, keep my heart firm upon Your religion."(Hadith, Tirmidhi)

Appendix F: 10 Healing Affirmations for the Journey Ahead

(Readers can whisper these to themselves, write them in journals, or post them on mirrors for daily strength.)

1. "I am not alone in my struggle. Mercy surrounds me, even when I cannot see it."

2. "Pain is not a punishment. It is a passage — and I am allowed to walk through it gently."

3. "Hope still lives in me, even on the days I cannot feel it."

4. "Every breath I take is proof that new chances are unfolding."

5. "My heart is stronger than my sadness."

6. "Healing is not a race. It is a path, and every small step matters."

7. "I am not defined by my darkest moment. I am defined by my light — even if it flickers."

8. "I am allowed to grieve, to heal, and to grow at my own pace."

9. "My life is a trust. My soul was created for goodness, even when I feel broken."

10. "I choose to stay. I choose to hope. I trust that better days are being written for me."

Appendix F: Guided Affirmation Exercise: Breathing Hope Back In

Pause, breathe, and say these words slowly and gently.

Step 1: Settle

- Find a quiet place if you can.

- Sit comfortably.

- Close your eyes or soften your gaze.

Step 2: Breathe

- Take a slow, deep breath in through your nose.

- Hold for a few seconds.

- Gently exhale through your mouth.

Repeat 3 times.

Feel your shoulders drop, your heart soften.

Step 3: Whisper or Think These Affirmations

(One line per breath.)

"I breathe in mercy... I breathe out fear."
"I breathe in hope... I breathe out despair."
"I breathe in light... I breathe out darkness."
"I breathe in healing... I breathe out hurt."
"I breathe in patience... I breathe out panic."
"I breathe in God's closeness... I breathe out loneliness."

Step 4: Silent Prayer

In your heart, say:

"O God, gather my scattered heart, heal what is broken within me, and let hope live in me again."

You Are Still Here.

You Are Still Breathing.

You Are Still Becoming.

You are not alone. This storm will pass.

Your story is not finished yet.

Reminder:

This exercise can be done in just 2–3 minutes, anytime the reader feels overwhelmed, lost, or tired. It gives an emotional reset while rooting them in remembrance, calm, and self-compassion.

Stay Connected

- Sign up to receive gentle healing tools, journaling prompts, and faith-based reflections — free resources created to help you rebuild hope, one day at a time.

Your heart deserves mercy.

Your journey deserves light.

You were never walking alone — and you never will be.

Because even the smallest whisper of hope can save a life.

A Note to Your Heart

If you are reading this,

it means you stayed.

You carried your heart through heavy nights.

You chose hope when despair tried to steal it away.

You chose mercy — for yourself, for your story, for your future.

Please remember:

Your survival is not small.

Your pain is not invisible.

Your hope is not foolish.

Even when the road feels long, even when the storms return, you are walking toward a mercy bigger than your fears — a mercy written for you by the One who loved you before you ever knew how to love yourself.

You never walked alone.

And you never will be.

Stay. Hope. Heal.

Your story is still being written — and it is more beautiful than you can imagine.

Appendix G: Support Sheet: How to Talk to a Loved One Who Is Suicidal

What You Can Say

Here are words that can help open the door to healing:

- "I'm here for you, no matter what. You're not alone."

- "You don't have to go through this by yourself. Can we talk?"

- "It's okay to feel overwhelmed. I care about you and want to help."

- "Have you been thinking about hurting yourself?"

- "Can we find someone together who knows how to help—like a counselor or therapist?"

What to Avoid Saying

Even with good intentions, certain phrases may do harm:

- "You have so much to live for."

- "Other people have it worse."

- "Just snap out of it."

- "That's selfish."

- "Don't talk like that."

Instead, focus on listening, validating, and connecting them to help.

How to Be a Good Listener

- Be present. Sit with them. Don't interrupt.

- Show empathy, not judgment.

- Use gentle silence to give them space to share.

- Nod or respond with short phrases: "That sounds hard," "I hear you."

What to Do in a Crisis

If someone is actively suicidal or has a plan:

- Stay with them. Don't leave them alone.

- Remove harmful items (pills, weapons, etc.) if you can do so safely.

- Call 911 or go to the nearest emergency room if there's immediate danger.

- Call/text 988 (U.S.) – The Suicide & Crisis Lifeline is available 24/7.

You can call on their behalf or together.

Follow Up and Support After

- Check in often: Send a text, drop by, or make a call.

- Offer practical help: Help schedule appointments, go with them, bring food, etc.

- Encourage professional support: Therapy, medical care, faith leaders, or peer support.

- Be patient: Healing takes time. Your presence matters more than perfect words.

Remember

You are not their therapist, but you can be their bridge to safety. Your love, presence, and concern may be the very thing that helps them stay.

References

Centers for Disease Control and Prevention. "Suicide Data and Statistics." Accessed April 2025. https://www.cdc.gov/suicide

National Institute of Mental Health. "Suicide Prevention." Accessed April 2025. https://www.nimh.nih.gov

The Trevor Project. *2023 National Survey on LGBTQ Youth Mental Health.* Accessed April 2025. https://www.thetrevorproject.org

Harvard T.H. Chan School of Public Health. "Religion and Suicide: Protective Factors in Faith-Based Practice." 2020. https://www.hsph.harvard.edu

Substance Abuse and Mental Health Services Administration. "Suicide Prevention." Accessed April 2025. https://www.samhsa.gov

World Health Organization. *Suicide Worldwide in 2019: Global Health Estimates.* Accessed April 2025. https://www.who.int

World Population Review. "Suicide Rates by Country (2023)." Accessed April 2025. https://worldpopulationreview.com

The Qur'an. Translated by Sahih International.

Al-Bukhari, Muhammad ibn Isma'il. *Sahih al-Bukhari.* Translated by M. Muhsin Khan.

Yaqeen Institute for Islamic Research. "Suicide, Mental Illness, and Islam." Accessed April 2025. https://yaqeeninstitute.org

Burkhart, Jessica. *Life Inside My Mind: 31 Authors Share Their Personal Struggles.* New York: Simon Pulse, 2018.

American Psychological Association. "Understanding Suicide." Accessed April 2025. https://www.apa.org

Chisolm, Margaret S, *From Survive to Thrive,* Maryland: John Hopkins University Press, 2021.

Esherick, Joan, *The Silent Cry: Teen Suicide and Self -Destructive Behaviors,* Philadephia: Mason Crest Publishers, 2005,

Acknowledgments

All praise is due to God —

the One who lifts broken hearts,

the One who brings light after darkness,

the One who answers the silent prayers we never knew how to speak.

If there is any goodness in this book, it is from Him.

If there are any shortcomings, they are from my own human limits.

To every heart who finds these pages —

You are not alone. You are not forgotten.

Your survival, your healing, your hope — it matters more than you know.

To the ones who prayed for me, supported me, believed in this vision before it had words —

your du'as (prayers) are stitched into every chapter.

May God reward you with blessings seen and unseen.

To those who feel invisible in their struggle —

this book was written for you.

May you always find a hand to hold, a light to follow, and a lifeline back to hope.

And finally, to God —

the Turner of hearts, the Writer of destinies, the Giver of life and light —

I entrust this work to You.

Accept it, purify it, multiply its mercy, and make it a means of nearness to You.

Ameen.

www.alyusra.com

Islamic Mental Health Solutions.

www.ingramcontent.com/pod-product-compliance
Lightning Source LLC
Chambersburg PA
CBHW061701120626
46550CB00003B/1034